SPAN[

A History

Copyright © 2022 by Hourly History.

All rights reserved.

Table of Contents

Introduction

The Catholic Monarchs

Reconquista: Ousting the Muslims

The New World

Spanish Control in the Americas

The Habsburgs

Treasure Fleets and Poverty

Pacific Exploration

The Bourbons

Napoleon: The Spanish Ulcer

The Fall of the Spanish Empire

Conclusion

Bibliography

Introduction

The Iberian Peninsula, the area of southwestern Europe that includes present-day Spain and Portugal, had a tumultuous early history. In the sixth century BCE, much of this area was conquered by the Carthaginians, an empire that originated in present-day Tunisia. From their capital, *Carthago Nova* (New Carthage, present-day Cartagena, Spain), the Carthaginians ruled a great portion of the region and established valuable silver mines and farming areas. Then, around 218 BCE, Spain was conquered by Rome, and within two hundred years, it became the Roman province of Hispania.

As the Roman Empire diminished in the fifth century CE, the peninsula was occupied by successive waves of Germanic conquerors, including the Vandals, the Visigoths, and the Alans. Then, in 711, a Muslim Umayyad leader, Tariq ibn Ziyad, landed at present-day Gibraltar and, over the course of an eight-year campaign, conquered all but the northernmost territory in the peninsula. The Iberian Peninsula thus became an autonomous Muslim caliphate known as al-Andalus. By the eighth century, al-Andalus had become one of the most powerful states in Europe, and Christian areas in the peninsula were reduced to a number of small, feuding polities in the north.

Al-Andalus remained powerful up to the eleventh century, with some of its major cities growing to exceed populations of 100,000 people. It became not just a military power but a renowned center of learning and culture. However, in the twelfth and thirteenth centuries, al-Andalus became weakened following a series of internal conflicts and continuing wars with the Christian kingdoms in the north. Gradually, the frontier between the Muslim caliphate and the Christian kingdoms moved south as larger parts of the peninsula fell under Christian rule.

For the first time in its history, the Iberian Peninsula began to move toward becoming a single autonomous kingdom ruled by its indigenous people. In a surprisingly short time, what is now called Spain would not only be a single country, but it would create the largest empire the world had ever seen.

Chapter One

The Catholic Monarchs

"Whose deeds can be compared with those of Spain? Not even the ancient Greeks and Romans."

—Francisco Xeres

The foundation of what would become the Spanish Empire came about not through war or conquest but following a wedding and the publication of a grammar book.

The languages spoken by the people who lived in the Iberian Peninsula had their roots in Roman Latin. By the fifteenth century, they had become a family of similar but not identical languages spoken by the inhabitants of a number of Christian kingdoms in the north. These included the Kingdoms of Castile, Leon, Aragon, Navarra, and Portugal. Each kingdom was, in effect, a separate country with its own culture and history and a language that was similar yet notably different to those spoken by people in the other kingdoms.

That began to change in 1492 with the publication of the *Gramática de la Lengua Castellana*, a grammar book that set out in writing for the first time how the language in the Iberian Peninsula should be written and spoken. This book was written by a poet, Antonio de Nebrija, and it was the first published grammar study of any modern European language. The same author followed up this feat three years later with the very first dictionary of the Spanish language.

A grammar book may not seem very dramatic today, but in 1492, it was truly revolutionary. Each Iberian kingdom up to that time had its own version of the Spanish language, all based on a common Latin root but all sufficiently different that they encouraged the inhabitants of each kingdom to regard themselves as different from the others. This first attempt to create a unified Spanish language not only made communications between the kingdoms easier, but it encouraged those who lived in the Iberian Peninsula to regard themselves, for the first time, as one people.

By the fifteenth century, the two most powerful Christian kingdoms in northern Spain were Aragon and Castile (permanently unified with Leon since the thirteenth century). The Basque Kingdom of Navarre and the Kingdom of Portugal were still in existence at this time, but neither was as powerful as Aragon or Castile which dominated most of the territory in present-day Spain. By the same time, the Muslim south, al-Andalus, had been reduced to a single caliphate centered in the city of Granada.

The ruler of Castile at this time was Henry IV. However, Henry was childless (he was also known as Henry the Impotent), and he was keen to use his younger half-sister, Isabella, to prop up his own rule and to secure alliances that would benefit Castile. From the age of six, Isabella was betrothed to a succession of prospective husbands from other Spanish kingdoms and even from the Kingdom of France, an ally of Castile.

Finally, in 1469, after a series of secret negotiations, Isabella was married to Ferdinand, the son of King John II of Aragon. However, Isabella and Ferdinand were second cousins, and the marriage would only be legal if special dispensation was received from the pope. With the help of Cardinal Rodrigo Borgia (who would later become Pope Alexander VI), a papal bull was issued in 1469 by Pope Pius II authorizing the marriage. The inconvenient fact that Pius II had actually died five years earlier did not seem to have unduly concerned anyone, and this marriage would become the basis of the creation of the Kingdom of Spain.

Castile and Aragon remained separate kingdoms, at least on paper, but with this marriage, the two most powerful polities in the Iberian Peninsula effectively acted together. In 1474, King Henry IV of Castile died, and Isabella became both queen of Castile and queen consort of Aragon. However, a dispute over this succession led to war with the Kingdom of Portugal. This dragged on for five years and resulted in a Castilian victory on land but a victory for Portugal at sea.

An uneasy peace between the warring kingdoms in 1479 allowed Isabella and Ferdinand to begin to look south toward the last vestige of the once-mighty al-Andalus, the Emirate of Granada.

Chapter Two

Reconquista: Ousting the Muslims

"Wrath gives ingenuity to the defeated man, but it leaves him in misery."

—Isabella I of Castile

The gradual process of bringing back Muslim lands in the Iberian Peninsula under Christian control had been ongoing for more than two hundred years. This series of battles and conquests became known as the *Reconquista*, and gradually, the frontier between al-Andalus and the kingdoms of the Christian north had been pushed south. The Christian assault on the Muslim lands had led to the capture of the main Muslim city in the region, Cordoba, in 1236. Ten years later, the ruler of the Emirate of Granada was forced to accept the status of a tributary state to the Kingdom of Castile. Each year, gold from present-day Mali and Burkina Faso was transferred to Castile from the treasury of Granada.

The Christian north and the Muslim south were notionally at peace, but for the next two hundred years, there were a series of minor conflicts on the frontier. Some originated from Castile, some from Granada, but the peace that existed was never stable or truly peaceful. Castile seized territory from Granada after victory in the Battle of Teba in 1330, and Granada supported a full-scale invasion of Castile at the Battle of Río Salado in 1340. Neither led to a substantial change in the frontier, and Granada continued to control a great deal of the southern coast of present-day Spain. Then, in 1481, Granada launched a full-scale assault on the Castilian frontier town of Zahara. Isabella and Ferdinand responded with a war against the Muslims that would last for ten years and lead to Christian control of all of present-day Spain.

At a time when most wars were short and often spontaneous, Isabella and Ferdinand took an unusually systematic approach to the war with Granada. This was a region with a strong military presence protected by mountains and other natural barriers, and the war was not a continuous series of battles but rather a series of separate campaigns. Each spring and summer, a new location would be the subject of an integrated Christian assault, and in winter, troops would retire to prepare for the next assault.

Isabella and Ferdinand also recruited professional mercenary soldiers from all over Europe to bolster their armies. They bought in the latest military hardware from around Europe, including the most powerful cannon available, capable of smashing enemy fortifications. Then, they directed the army they had created to begin a systematic reduction of the main Islamic strongholds. In addition to the city of Granada itself, these comprised an interlocking network of fortresses, fortified towns, and watchtowers occupying commanding positions in the hills and mountains of the present-day Spanish region of Andalusia.

One important factor in the final outcome of this war was that, for the first time, the Kingdoms of Castile and Aragon were truly unified and combined their resources. In previous conflicts, the Christian kingdoms had acted independently and had often broken off wars against the Muslims to protect themselves from attacks by other Christian kingdoms. During this war, Castile provided most of the troops and the funds, while Aragon provided naval support and military hardware including cannons. Aristocrats in both kingdoms were offered incentives in the form of land and titles for taking part in this war, and both Isabella and Ferdinand used the war to consolidate their positions.

On the other side, the Nasrid ruler of the Emirate of Granada, Emir Abu-l-Hasan Ali, faced internal dissent as well as potential attacks from other Muslim kingdoms in North Africa. For these reasons, Granada proved unable to resist the systematic and carefully planned campaign mounted by Castile and Aragon.

The campaign began in the western area of the Emirate. The town of Alhama de Granada was taken in 1482, as Ferdinand took personal control of the attacking armies. The next target for the Christian armies was the city of Loja. The initial siege failed, but the son of the emir, Boabdil, who led the relief force, rebelled against his father and announced that he was now Emir Muhammad XII. In 1483, the new emir was captured by Christian forces after the Battle of Lucena. Shrewdly, Ferdinand chose to release his prisoner, noting in a letter, "To put Granada in division and destroy it we have decided to free him. He has to make war on his father."

Faced with internal dissent and insurrection, the Muslim armies suffered a series of defeats. The city of Rhonda was taken in 1485 after an extensive bombardment with cannons. Marbella, a major base for Granada's navy, fell soon thereafter, followed by Malaga in 1487. In 1489, Christian forces began a long siege of the only remaining Muslim stronghold outside Granada, the city of Baza. Morale amongst the attackers faltered during the siege, and Isabella came to Baza herself to prove additional motivation. When Baza finally fell after six months, only the city of Granada itself remained.

The siege of that city began in April 1491, and the city finally surrendered in January 1492. The Emirate of Granada was no more, and the combined forces of Castile and Aragon under the dual rule of Isabella and Ferdinand effectively controlled most of the Iberian Peninsula. For the first time, Ferdinand was referred to as the king of Spain and Isabella as the queen of Spain. Most historians take this date as marking the true beginning of Spain as a nation.

During the war with Granada, the army controlled by Castile and Aragon had developed to become an effective and efficient force—well-equipped, well-led, and capable of using advanced military tactics that would lead to it becoming one of the most formidable military forces in Europe. In the course of little more than ten years, Spain had been transformed from a collection of individual polities into a single powerful nation.

Just before the fall of Granada, Queen Isabella had received a visitor in the nearby town of Santa Fe. This man wanted funding for a bold voyage across the Atlantic Ocean in order to find a new sea route to the Orient. To most people, this seemed impossible, and the man, who had been seeking support for this voyage for a number of years, was dismissed as a lunatic. On the advice of her confessor, Isabella also turned him down. Then, it seems that Ferdinand also heard about the man's plans and persuaded his wife to change her mind. A royal guard was sent to fetch the man, who had left the city, and he was brought back to hear the good news.

The man's name was Christopher Columbus, and he would help to transform the new nation of Spain into the largest and most powerful the world had ever seen.

Chapter Three

The New World

"We came to serve God and to get rich, as all men wish to do."

—Bernal Diaz del Castillo

Relatively little is known of the early life of Christopher Columbus. He was born in Genoa on the northwestern coast of Italy in 1451 and seems to have gone to sea at a young age, taking part in voyages as far as Britain and as far south as Ghana. In 1479, he married a Portuguese noblewoman, Filipa Moniz Perestrelo, and he then lived in Lisbon for a number of years. There he studied astronomy, geography, and history and became fascinated by the spice trade, then one of the most lucrative trades in the world.

Spices such as pepper, cinnamon, cassia, ginger, and nutmeg were extremely popular in Europe but could only be cultivated in Southeast Asia. Importing goods from that region to Europe involved long overland routes that used the Silk

Road, the main trading route between Asia and Europe. The Byzantine Empire had controlled much of this trade, but the fall of their capital, Constantinople, in 1453 meant that the Ottoman Empire was able to seize control of the spice trade. Additional taxes and tariffs made spices even more expensive, and many European explorers sought to find an alternate maritime route to bring spices back to Europe without passing through the territory of the Ottoman Empire.

Most were looking for a route to the east, but Christopher Columbus believed that there was another way. He came to believe that it would be possible to reach India by sailing west from Europe across the Atlantic Ocean. Contrary to popular belief, people in the fifteenth century did not think that the Earth was flat. Navigators and geographers understood that the Earth was a sphere and that it would be possible to reach India from Europe by sailing either east or west. Of course, there were no world maps then, and Columbus would have had no idea that a western voyage to India would be longer and more hazardous than a voyage on the eastern route.

In reality, a journey to Asia by sailing west from Europe would have involved crossing the

Atlantic, rounding Cape Horn, and then crossing the mighty Pacific Ocean. Columbus estimated that Japan was around 2,400 miles (3,800 kilometers) from the west coast of Europe; the actual distance is more than 10,000 miles (16,000 kilometers). Although Columbus' calculations were entirely wrong, he did know that vast wealth would be available to any person who did find an alternate sea route to India and to any nation that funded such a voyage.

Columbus was not a wealthy man, and he needed funding for his planned voyage. For several years, he pitched his idea to rulers in Spain, France, Portugal, and England. His plans were rejected as impractical, and no nation agreed to fund such a voyage. When he first approached Isabella and Ferdinand in 1486, both were much too busy with the war against the Emirate of Granada to spend much time considering his offer. When he came back with a revised version of his plan in January 1492, the war was almost over, and the city of Granada was about to fall. Both Isabella and Ferdinand were considering how to improve the fortunes of their new kingdom after the war, and Columbus' proposal received a more sympathetic hearing.

Most people were skeptical about his ideas, and few believed he would succeed, but the potential rewards if he was correct were astronomical. After initial doubts, Isabella agreed to fund a voyage with three ships and with Columbus as the leader of an expedition. The contract concluded with Columbus was very, very generous. He would be given new titles, including viceroy and governor of any new lands he might claim for Spain, and he would be given 10% of all revenues from those lands in perpetuity. Isabella and Ferdinand agreed to these terms, it seems, because—like most people—they thought there was very little chance that Columbus would succeed and a very high probability that he would die during the voyage.

On August 3, 1492, Columbus left Spain in his fleet of three small ships. On October 12, his crew spotted land which he believed to be the coast of India. He was, of course, completely wrong. What he had arrived at was an island of the Bahamas, located east of and between present-day Cuba and Florida. Columbus and his men explored several other islands in what they named the West Indies, still believing that they had reached Asia.

Although he found no spices, Columbus did find something even more interesting: gold. He noted that many of the tribes that he encountered wore gold earrings and other body ornaments. Clearly, gold was plentiful in this region, though he was not able to find its source on his first voyage. When he arrived back in Spain in March 1493, he was given a hero's welcome and granted an audience with Isabella and Ferdinand. They were very interested in his report, and between 1493 and 1504, Columbus made three more voyages of exploration to this new region on behalf of Spain.

Isabella was deeply religious and truly seems to have believed that the so-called "savages" encountered by Columbus presented a remarkable opportunity to spread Christianity by evangelizing to these people. Pope Alexander VI agreed, issuing a papal decree in May 1493, which gave Spain and Portugal the exclusive rights to exploit new lands in the west, with the proviso that they must also ensure the spread of Christianity. Ferdinand and others seemed primarily interested in more pragmatic and less spiritual matters, namely Columbus' belief that this new region represented a rich source of gold.

With these new discoveries and the issue of the papal decree, Spain was set to transition from a single nation-state into a vast empire.

Chapter Four

Spanish Control in the Americas

"I continued to burn and demolish the towers of their idols and their houses. That they might become more sensible of their situation."

—Hernan Cortes

In 1506, Columbus died, still believing that he had discovered a western route to Asia. This misperception carried on after his death, with all the indigenous people that Spanish explorers encountered in the Americas being referred to as *Indios* (Indians) and the new lands described as the West Indies.

For two decades after Columbus' discovery, Spanish and Portuguese explorers made many voyages to the Caribbean. There, they began a policy of ruthless exploitation that would be repeated throughout their discovery of South and Central America. One of the first Spanish settlements was on a large island they named Hispaniola (now divided into the Dominican Republic and Haiti). The indigenous people there, the Taino, were put to work as little more than slaves, working shallow gold mines and in early sugar cane plantations.

Working and living conditions for these people under Spanish rule were brutal. These people had also not been exposed to diseases such as smallpox and cholera before, which the incomers brought with them, and had no immunity. Thousands died, and even diseases such as measles, which was rarely fatal for Europeans, proved to be lethal for the Taino. Within no more than 15 years, the entire native population of Hispaniola, which may have amounted to hundreds of thousands of people, had been effectively wiped out. Faced with a shortage of labor, the Spanish began raiding nearby islands, including present-day Cuba, Jamaica, and Puerto Rico, to capture more slaves. These too died in large numbers, and the diseases the Spanish had brought also spread to those islands. By this time, the Spanish Crown granted a license to allow for enslaved people to be brought directly from Africa to work in the New World.

In the early years of the sixteenth century, the Spanish continued to explore and occupy islands in the Caribbean. Then, in 1519, a Spanish settler in Cuba, Hernan Cortes, was given permission to explore part of the mainland in present-day Mexico. Cortes encountered the Aztec Empire, a confederation of indigenous people, but he also found vast quantities of gold. The Spanish *conquistadores* (conquerors) were vastly outnumbered by indigenous warriors, but they brought with them new military technology originally developed for Spain during the war with Granada, including metal body armor, cannons, and firearms. Against this new technology, the weapons and tactics of the local people were almost completely ineffective.

At the Battle of Otumba in 1520, for example, a Spanish force of fewer than 1,000 men under the command of Cortes fought with an Aztec army that numbered at least 20,000 warriors. The outcome was the total defeat of the Aztec army, while Spanish casualties amounted to no more than 70 men killed. No one knows how many Aztecs died in battle, but it certainly must have been hundreds, if not thousands. Soon after, the main Aztec city of Tenochtitlan fell to the Spanish, and the Aztec emperor, Moctezuma II, was killed. By 1532, virtually all the territory in present-day Mexico that had been ruled by the Aztec Empire was brought under Spanish rule.

With the defeat of the Aztecs, the Spanish turned their attention to the only other major empire in South America, the Incas, located in present-day Peru. The Incas were more powerful and their empire larger than that of the Aztecs, but they suffered from the same disadvantages when facing troops using the latest in European military technology. At the Battle of Cajamarca in 1532, another Spanish conquistador, Francisco Pizarro, led another small Spanish army against the Incas. The Incas were defeated, and their emperor, Atahualpa, was captured by the Spanish. It would take another forty years before the last Inca stronghold in Vilcabamba was occupied, but after this battle, the final outcome was never in doubt.

By 1567, Spanish conquistadors had occupied most of the continent of South America, including the present-day nations of Argentina, Bolivia, Chile, Colombia, Ecuador, Paraguay, Peru, Uruguay, and Venezuela. In most of these areas, their main objective was the acquisition of gold and silver. Initially, they would plunder the gold and silver artifacts created by the people they conquered. Then, they established gold, silver, and precious stone mines, mainly worked by enslaved indigenous people.

Even by modern standards, the amount of plunder that these explorers brought back to Spain was staggering. Between 1504 and 1522, over 500 Spanish ships made the voyage to South America—450 survived to make the return journey, each bringing with it unimaginable riches. From 1522 on, the number of Spanish ships making the voyage to and from the New World increased steadily. In Seville, the *Casa de Contratación* (House of Trade) was established in 1503. Every Spanish ship that made the voyage to America had to be licensed through this government organization, and every returning ship had to report its cargo.

Initially, the Spanish Crown took 50% of every returning cargo, though eventually this was reduced first to 30% and then to 10%. No one is entirely certain how much treasure the Spanish took from the Americas. Up to 1560, this may have amounted to over 200 metric tons of gold and anything up to 10,000 metric tons of silver, plus an unknown quantity of precious stones. What we do know is that Spanish control of America caused vast wealth to flow into Spain during the sixteenth century. The largest proportion went to the Crown, smaller amounts went to the Church, and individual traders and explorers became vastly wealthy.

Spain was only created in the late fifteenth century, but this continuing influx of treasure from America made it one of the wealthiest European nations during the sixteenth century. However, in the early years of the sixteenth century, the monarchy of Spain changed fundamentally.

Chapter Five

The Habsburgs

"I came, I saw, God conquered."

—Charles I of Spain

Queen Isabella died in 1504 and was succeeded as the queen of Castile by her daughter, Joanna (now remembered as Joanna the Mad). At the time of her ascension to the throne, Joanna was married to Philip the Handsome, Archduke of Austria and a member of the House of Habsburg. This was an arranged marriage created in the hope of securing a military alliance with the Holy Roman Empire that was intended to provide mutual protection against the growing power of France. At the same time that Joanna became queen, her father, King Ferdinand of Aragon, proclaimed himself to also be governor and administrator of Castile. In July 1506, Philip the Handsome was proclaimed to be king of Castile, but only a few months later, he died. This pushed Spain into a period of turmoil and revolt.

Ferdinand was said to have been very unhappy with the declaration of Philip as king of Castile, and there were unproven rumors that he had Philip poisoned. After the death of Philip, Ferdinand persuaded his daughter to hand all power over to him, and he effectively became king of both Aragon and Castile. In 1509, he had Joanna confined in the Royal Convent in Tordesillas, where she would spend the rest of her life. The official order making this possible noted that Joanna was "insane," though there are suspicions that this was untrue and that it was done simply to ensure that Ferdinand could rule both Castile and Aragon unopposed. When Ferdinand died in 1516, his successor was Joanna and Philip's son, 17-year-old Charles I. It was decided that Charles and Joanna would rule as co-monarchs, though as Joanna continued to be confined in Tordesillas due to her supposed madness, by 1509, Charles was effectively king of both Castile and Aragon.

However, having a Habsburg king ruling over Spain met with a great deal of internal resistance. The Habsburgs were one of the oldest aristocratic families in Europe; Habsburg Castle was built in what was then the Duchy of Swabia (present-day Switzerland) in the eleventh century. The

Habsburgs also formed one of the principal sovereign dynasties of Europe from the fifteenth to the twentieth century. Members of this family served as kings of Austria, Hungary, and Bohemia as well as emperors of the Holy Roman Empire, a confederation of German states.

The Habsburgs were one of the most powerful families in Europe, but they were of Austrian descent and had no prior connection with Spain. Many Spanish people regarded Charles I as a foreigner even though he was the son of a Spanish queen, and some were very unhappy about his becoming king of the most important territories of Spain. He had been raised in the Netherlands, and when he first arrived in Spain, he spoke almost no Spanish.

In 1519, Charles was also elected as Holy Roman Emperor following the death of his grandfather, Maximillian I. This simply increased the feeling within Spain that the country was ruled by a foreign king who had no direct connection with the country. In 1520, this situation prompted what would become known as the Revolt of the Comuneros (Communities), where large parts of Castile were taken over by rebels who sought to depose Charles. The revolt was finally crushed at the Battle of Villalar in

1521. Charles' position as king and the right of Habsburgs to rule Spain were thereby confirmed.

In 1556, Charles abdicated in favor of his son, Philip II, and until 1700, Spain would be ruled by a series of Habsburg monarchs. Under Habsburg rule, Spain followed a consistent policy that was focused on several main aims: 1) The defense of the Catholic Church and the authority of the pope against the Protestant Reformation. 2) Support for the Holy Roman Empire, particularly against a Muslim threat from the Ottoman Empire. 3) Spreading Catholic Christianity to the indigenous people of the Americas and protecting that region from exploitation by other European nations. 4) Opposing the growing power of France.

Under Habsburg rule, Spain became one of the most powerful states in Europe, both militarily and politically. With the riches that continued to flow from Spanish possessions in the Americas, Spain also became a center of culture and the arts. During what became known as the Spanish Golden Age, writers such as Miguel de Cervantes and artists including Diego Velazquez and El Greco became world-renowned. However, another less pleasant aspect of Habsburg rule also became widely known and feared: the Inquisition.

This department of the Spanish Church had been formed under Isabella, but during the reign of Philip II, its power increased dramatically. Spanish students were forbidden to travel abroad (other than to Spanish-controlled territory), the importation of books was forbidden, and the Inquisition became responsible for the censorship of all publications within Spain and the hunting of suspected heretics.

The period of Habsburg rule over Spain was also a time of almost continuous warfare. During the seventeenth century, Spain was involved in long-term wars with Portugal (1640-1668), France (1635-1659), Italy (1628-1631), and, most destructive of all, the Thirty Years' War (1618-1648). This latter war remains one of the most lethal ever fought in Europe, accounting for the deaths of up to eight million soldiers and civilians through combat, famine, and disease. Even the flow of riches coming from the Americas could not prevent the Spanish treasury from declining to the edge of bankruptcy in the face of almost constant conflict.

Chapter Six

Treasure Fleets and Poverty

"I would rather lose all my lands and a hundred lives than be king over heretics."

—Philip II of Spain

The flow of gold and silver from the Americas to Spain that began in the early sixteenth century had a number of unexpected consequences. At first, this led to what seemed to be a never-ending flow of riches into the Spanish treasury (by the end of the sixteenth century, during the reign of Philip II, gold and silver from the Americas accounted for more than 25% of the total national revenue). This wealth prompted policies of aggressive military expansion within Spain, using wealth from the Americas to purchase military equipment and to pay for huge armies and a series of wars.

Yet even this flow of wealth was not sufficient to fund the military ambitions of the Habsburg kings, particularly Charles and Philip II. Believing that wealth from the Americas would continue to flow to Spain, both kings borrowed on an unprecedented scale, confident that all debts could be settled with American gold and silver in the future. However, the influx of gold and silver into Spain had one unforeseen consequence. As more and more American gold and silver entered the Spanish economy, this undermined the existing currency, causing inflation. Even as the conquests of Peru and Mexico were being completed, prices in Spain were rising, and by 1560, prices of most commodities across Spain had doubled. Inflation spread to Europe, causing what would become known as the price revolution of the sixteenth century. Even as more and more gold and silver flowed to Spain from the Americas, inflation meant that it was progressively worth less and less.

The cost of maintaining Spanish territories in the Americas was also vast. A huge fleet of ships was required to transport people and supplies to the New World and to bring back gold and silver. Warships were needed to protect these ships from attack by England and other maritime nations. Troops were needed to oversee the indigenous people in the Americas, and a vast (and expensive) bureaucracy was required to control and administrate these colonies. Many of the ablest soldiers chose to go to the Americas, where it was possible for an individual to become very wealthy. As a result, when Spain became involved in a series of wars in Europe, more troops were needed, and these were often created through the use of paid mercenaries, another drain on the Spanish treasury.

By the sixteenth century, almost all the wealth from the Americas was being used to service debts and to pay for armies engaged in warfare in Europe. Almost none of the gold and silver from America was being invested in growing industry and commerce within Spain. This was apparent to some people at the time. As early as 1600, Martin Gonzalez de Cellorigo, an *arbitrista* (a group of reformist social commentators), noted that "The effect of an apparently endless flow of American silver into Seville had been to create a false sense of wealth as consisting of gold and silver, whereas true wealth lay in productive investment."

This simple fact was clearly not apparent to the Habsburg kings who ruled Spain throughout the sixteenth century. Instead of reinvesting the wealth from the Americas within Spain, they continued to spend it on a series of European wars that brought little real benefit. As the century progressed and their levels of debt increased, they resorted to increasingly complex and risky loans. To bring more money into the national treasury, taxes were increased on almost all goods. This had a direct impact on the poorest people and had the effect of stifling commerce and business within Spain. Inflation within Spain and increasing taxes made exports to other countries very difficult. The export of merino wool, for example, which had formerly been a significant source of revenue for Spain, declined sharply in the face of cheaper alternatives coming from England and the Netherlands. As a result, Spanish commerce and agriculture declined further. While wealth continued to flow, this simply meant that Spain needed to import more and more goods from other countries.

Then, the seemingly limitless supply of gold and silver began to decline. Between 1590 and 1600, bullion worth almost 14 million pesos reached Spain from the Americas. Between 1630 and 1641, this dropped to 7 million pesos, and from 1651 to 1660, it had declined to barely 2 million. The expansionist plans of the Spanish Habsburg kings (and the vast debts they accumulated to support these) were based on a continuing supply of wealth from the Americas. When the mines there began to run down, the effect on the Spanish economy was disastrous.

At the beginning of the sixteenth century, Spain was one of the most powerful and wealthy nations in the world. By the end of the seventeenth century, it was virtually bankrupt. Once-prosperous industrial cities such as Granada, Segovia, and Toledo fell into decline. In Castile, in particular, increasing taxes and the effects of inflation had severely impacted agriculture. The windfall that came from the import of bullion from the Americas to Spain had not brought long-term wealth and power. Instead, it caused hubris, a fatal overconfidence that led to expansionist military plans while failing to invest in Spanish infrastructure and commerce. No longer the most powerful nation in Europe, Spain had been overtaken by France, and French culture and art came to dominate.

Nevertheless, even while these fundamental changes were sweeping Spain, it was still funding exploration and conquest in other parts of the world.

Chapter Seven

Pacific Exploration

"We have to discover the world."

—Spanish proverb

Not content with the exploitation of the Americas, Charles I ordered a new voyage of exploration in 1525 that overshadowed even the efforts of Christopher Columbus. Although the Americas produced gold and silver in vast quantities, they did not hold the very commodity that Columbus had set out to obtain for Spain: spice.

A Spanish expedition in 1522 led by Portuguese explorer Ferdinand Magellan had led to the first circumnavigation of the world. A new expedition in 1525, led by Spanish explorer Garcia Jofre de Loaisa, was to follow up on this and, most importantly, to survey and claim new lands for Spain. The most important objectives for the new expedition were the Spice Islands (present-day Maluku Islands, off the east coast of Indonesia). There was also an important secondary objective: the location of the island of Ophir, mentioned in the Bible as providing gold to King Solomon. Spanish geographers thought that this island might lie somewhere off the coast of China, and it was believed to be another potential source of bullion for the Spanish Crown.

Seven ships under the command of de Loaisa left Spain in July 1525. In May of the following year, four of these ships entered the Pacific Ocean (two others had been wrecked, and one had deserted the expedition and returned to Spain). Only one ship, the galleon *Santa Maria de la Victoria*, reached the Spice Islands in September after a truly epic voyage (de Loaisa himself died of scurvy before the ship reached its destination). This voyage began a period of Spanish exploration and colonization of territory in the Pacific.

In 1541, another Spanish explorer, Ruy Lopez de Villalobos, was commissioned by the viceroy of New Spain, Antonio de Mendoza, to undertake a voyage to the west from Mexico in search of the *Islas del Poniente* (Islands of the West). In February 1543, the fleet of six ships arrived in a bay they named Malaga (present-day Baganga Bay) on the east coast of the island of Mindanao. De Villalobos named the island Caesarea Karoli to honor Charles I, the king of Spain. In 1544, the expedition reached two islands (present-day Samar and Leyte) which were named *Las Islas Filipinas* (The Philippine Islands) to honor then-Prince Philip II. Further expeditions followed, and in 1571, Manila was declared to be the capital of the Philippine Islands and of all Spanish possessions in the region, collectively known as the Spanish East Indies.

In 1603, the Spanish added the island of Tidore, one of the Spice Islands, to the zone they controlled in this region. A survey of the coast of Japan was carried out by Spanish explorers in the early years of the seventeenth century, and King Philip II of Spain became one of the first European monarchs to send an ambassador to Japan. The last major expansion of Spanish territory in the Pacific occurred in 1668 when Jesuit missionary Diego Luis de San Vitores first established a Christian mission on the island of Guam. Four years later, San Vitores was killed by local people, sparking the Spanish-Chamorro Wars from 1672 to 1699.

Spanish troops and ships were sent to Guam and other islands in the Marianas chain. Over the course of several years, the native people on these islands were pacified by Spanish troops using the same brutal tactics that had proved so effective in America. Villages were destroyed, people imprisoned and executed, and whole populations moved to other islands to suit the needs of the Spanish. By the end of the seventeenth century, Spain controlled virtually all of the Mariana Islands. This represented the zenith of the Spanish Empire in terms of territorial acquisition.

Spain was still in control of most of Central and South America as well as parts of present-day Florida. These continued to provide bullion, but by the end of the seventeenth century, this had reduced to a trickle compared to the former torrent. Spain also indirectly controlled the Spanish Netherlands after the Habsburg family came to the throne in that area in 1556, as well as parts of Italy. Spanish acquisitions in the Pacific extended their power in that region, but none provided wealth to compare with that found in the early stages of the conquest of the Americas. The island of Ophir, the "Island of Gold," proved to be nothing more than a myth. Other legends of islands rich in gold, silver, and precious stones also proved to have no basis in reality.

By the end of the seventeenth century, the Spanish economy was in such a dire condition that simply providing the troops and ships needed to guard and supply these territories in Asia was almost too much. Funding new voyages of exploration in this region or even being required to take extensive military action was simply not a practical possibility. At that time, the ascension to the throne of Spain of a new sovereign house was to lead to a series of reforms that would transform Spain.

Chapter Eight

The Bourbons

"Every time I appoint someone to a vacant position, I make a hundred unhappy and one ungrateful."

—Louis XIV of France

In 1700, King Charles II of Spain died. He had no children and would be the last of the Spanish Habsburg kings. The succession of the next ruler would plunge Spain into another series of destructive and costly wars.

The principal claimant to the throne was a French prince, Philippe, the duke of Anjou. He was the grandson of Maria Theresa, a Spanish woman from a notable family who had married King Louis XIV of France. Because Charles II did not have a living heir, this meant that the actual heir apparent to the Spanish throne was Louis, the grand dauphin of France. However, it seemed that Louis would almost certainly become king of France when his father died, so instead,

Philippe, his younger brother, was nominated as the heir to Charles II.

This was contested by another possible heir and member of the Habsburg family, Charles of Austria. The proclamation in Spain as Philippe of Anjou as the new king in 1700 led to a bitter war between France and the Spanish Bourbons on one side and an alliance comprising the Dutch Republic, Britain, the Holy Roman Empire, and the Spanish Habsburgs on the other. What became known as the War of the Spanish Succession began in 1701 and raged until 1715.

The war was costly to all participants, and when it ended, Spain was forced to concede Gibraltar and the island of Menorca to the British and to give Britain increased trading rights in the Americas. They also lost the Spanish Netherlands and territories in Italy to Austria and Savoy. What they gained was Philippe of Anjou as King Philip V of Spain, and with his ascension, Bourbon kings would rule Spain for the next one hundred years.

During this war, Philip also undertook legal changes intended to turn Spain into a single nation. When he became king, the nation was still a confederation of individual kingdoms, notably Castile and Aragon. Angered by a lack of support for his cause within Aragon, Philip introduced a series of acts, the Nueva Planta decrees, which removed all legal distinctions between residents of Castile and Aragon and effectively meant that Castile ruled all of Spain. Madrid became the capital and center of administration and rule, and Castilian became the language of government. Other languages used in Spain, such as Catalan, were suppressed. These new acts can be seen as the point at which Spain truly became a single nation, but they caused anger in many areas and led to the War of the Spanish Succession dragging on longer and being more destructive than anyone could have foreseen.

Soon after the end of that civil war, Spain was involved in yet another war, the War of the Quadruple Alliance from 1718 to 1720), where it suffered a serious defeat at the hands of an alliance of Britain, Austria, France, and the Dutch Republic. After that, the Bourbon rulers of Spain decided to take a much more cautious approach, avoiding wars where possible and focusing instead on reforms within the country.

Philip V began his reign by strengthening the executive power of the monarchy. Previously, under the Habsburgs, power had been shared between the king and several councils of state.

Following the model of monarchy in France, the power and authority of these councils was reduced, and the king became the main arbiter of internal and foreign policy in Spain. The way in which Spanish territory in the Americas was administered was also streamlined and improved. Silver production from mines in the Americas, for example, more than tripled between 1700 and 1750.

However, the consolidation within the Spanish Empire was impacted by the Seven Years' War from 1756 to 1763, a global conflict during which Spain found itself in an alliance with France and fighting an opposing alliance led by Britain and Prussia. This led to a number of battles within Europe but also to conflict in the Americas and Asia, where France and Spain fought the forces of Britain. During this conflict, Spain lost the important port of Havana in Cuba as well as Manila in the Philippines to the British. The Treaty of Paris that ended the war in 1763 effectively ended Spain's monopoly in trading with the Americas and established Britain as the dominant naval and colonial power. Rather than further negatively impacting the Spanish economy, this actually led to notable improvements.

By the mid-1780s, there was significant commercial activity within Spain, notably in the textile business centered in Catalonia, which saw the first impact of industrialization. Increased productivity also affected Spain's possessions in the Americas, and the production of silver and sugar both continued to rise during this period. Even the Spanish army and navy, both of which had declined sharply in quality and size under the Habsburgs, began to recover. When the 13 British colonies in America declared independence in 1765, an event that led to the American Revolutionary War, the Bourbon kings of Spain concluded an alliance with Bourbon France to fight on behalf of the rebellious colonists in America. During the war, Spanish forces were able to occupy the British forts in the Bahamas, and West Florida was taken from the British.

Under Bourbon rule in the eighteenth century, it really seemed that Spain was making progress toward once again becoming a leading world power. As the century drew to a close, the Spanish possessions in the Americas were still vast and provided a regular source of much-needed funds to the Spanish economy. Spanish industry was, for the first time, showing signs of recovery and improvement though agriculture remained largely backward and primitive. However, events in France were about to alter the face of Europe in a wave of revolutionary fervor that would change everything.

Chapter Nine

Napoleon: The Spanish Ulcer

"Impossible is a word to be found only in the dictionary of fools."

—Napoleon Bonaparte

The Bourbon monarchy in France was one of the most entrenched systems of rule in Europe. This house had provided the kings of France for over 200 years, but in 1789, France was swept by a wave of political unrest that led to the deposition of King Louis XVI and his execution in 1793. The French Revolution led to a period of chaos and anarchy within the country and to a wave of fear sweeping across most other European countries. The revolution, based on the notions of *liberté*, *égalité*, and *fraternité* (liberty, equality, and fraternity), called for an end to the feudal system, the introduction of universal suffrage, and government through elected assemblies rather than by a monarch. These inventive new ideas were seen as a threat to the social systems and administration of virtually every other European nation, including Spain.

The revolution seemed to have ended when a French general, Napoleon Bonaparte, staged a coup in 1799. Napoleon appointed himself first consul and effectively became the dictator of France. Though some were suspicious of his motives, most saw this as a welcome end to the chaos that the revolution had brought. In 1802, the Treaty of Amiens brought to an end a series of wars fought by French revolutionary forces against other European nations. Two years later, Napoleon appointed himself emperor of France.

The Spanish Empire had formed an alliance with the new French Empire, and in 1804, the capture of a Spanish merchant convoy off Portugal by ships of the British Royal Navy led to a declaration of war by France and Spain on Britain. The combined Spanish and French navies outnumbered the British, but at the Battle of Trafalgar in 1805, the Spanish and French fleets were soundly defeated. In 1807, a French army transited through Spain to invade Portugal. The following year, though Spain and France were nominally still allies, French troops effectively took over the country. Napoleon forced the abdication of the Spanish king, Ferdinand VII, and announced that his brother, Joseph Bonaparte, was the new Spanish ruler. Spain effectively became little more than a province of the French Empire.

Although the Spanish Army was largely ineffective, the next six years saw a bloody guerilla war waged in Spain against the French occupiers and, under the command of Sir Arthur Wellesley (later the Duke of Wellington), a series of battles between French and British troops in what became known as the Peninsular War. The Spanish government was during this time reduced to the Cortes of Cadiz, a government in exile based in the besieged port of Cadiz. Centers of resistance to the French occupation formed around *juntas*, local emergency governments. When French forces were finally forced to withdraw from Spain in 1814, the country was left without an effective overall government, and the juntas became increasingly important to maintain order.

In 1812, the Cortes of Cádiz had established a new liberal Spanish constitution that called for the establishment of a constitutional monarchy and an elected government. When the French withdrew, most Spanish people assumed that this new constitution would form the basis of a new and more democratic nation. However, when King Ferdinand VII was back on the Spanish throne in 1814, one of his first acts was to repudiate the new constitution and declare a return to an absolutist monarchy. In 1820, a Spanish general, Rafael del Riego, staged a coup which reintroduced the constitution. Ferdinand was reluctantly forced to accept this. However, three years later, the restored Bourbon French king, Louis XVIII, raised an army and invaded Spain. The forces of the constitutional government were defeated, and once again, Ferdinand was established as the absolute ruler of Spain.

For the last ten years of his reign, before his death in 1833, Ferdinand oversaw the suppression of any political opposition to absolute rule and the crushing of revolts against his rule, most notably the War of the Agraviados, a wide-scale revolt that began in Catalonia in 1827 and spread to many other regions of Spain. After his death, Ferdinand was replaced as monarch by his daughter, Isabella II. Before long, changes that had begun during the war with Napoleon would lead to instability and internal conflict that would see the disintegration of the Spanish Empire and the descent of the nation into a series of destructive civil wars.

Chapter Ten

The Fall of the Spanish Empire

"Spain is a bottle of beer and I am the cork. When that comes out, all the liquid inside will escape, God knows in what direction."

—Ferdinand VII of Spain

The juntas that had become so powerful in Spain during the Napoleonic invasion were also established in many Spanish territories in the Americas. In the period after 1812, the governance of Spanish colonies was divided between royalists, who supported the absolute rule of Ferdinand VII, and those who supported the liberal, democratic constitution of 1812 (which had also recognized for the first time indigenous people living in Spanish colonies as Spanish citizens). One after another, Spanish territories in the Americas declared independence.

The first was Argentina in 1810. This was followed by Paraguay and Uruguay in 1811, Chile in 1818, and Colombia in 1819. In 1821, the single largest Spanish territory, Mexico, declared independence. Spain attempted to retake some of these territories after Ferdinand VII was re-established as absolute monarch in 1823, but the Spanish Army and Navy simply were not powerful enough to complete military campaigns in the Americas. After a failed attempt to invade Mexico in 1829, Spain was forced to accept that it no longer had control over their most important overseas source of wealth in the Americas. In 1836, the Spanish government finally announced that it would renounce sovereignty over all of its former colonies in America.

In Spain itself, the reign of Queen Isabella II was marked by turmoil and chaos. At the time of the death of Ferdinand VII, Isabella was just three years old. For seven years, Spain was wracked by a civil war between supporters of Isabella and those of another claimant to the throne, Ferdinand's brother, the Infante Carlos. His supporters, known as Carlists, supported a return to an absolute monarchy, while generally, those who supported Isabella wanted to see some form of constitutional rule.

What became known as the First Carlist War began in 1833 and continued until 1840. The war left up to 100,000 troops dead and brought famine and poverty to a large proportion of the Spanish people. The Carlists were defeated, but their dissatisfaction would remain, and Spain would see a Second Carlist War in 1846, which involved a revolt in Catalonia. This, too, was defeated.

Isabella was declared to be of age at 13 and formally became queen in 1843. Her reign was marked by a number of attempted coups and revolutions. She was finally deposed in 1868 following a revolution, but her son, Alfonso XII, would eventually become the constitutional monarch of Spain in 1874. When he died at the age of just 27 in 1885, he was succeeded by his son, Alfonso XIII, who would be the constitutional king of Spain well into the twentieth century. By that time, the last vestiges of the Spanish Empire had disappeared.

During Isabella II's reign, Spain launched a disastrous war to retake the Dominican Republic. The Dominican Restoration War of 1863 proved to be so expensive and caused so many casualties without a decisive result that it was abandoned after less than two years. Cuba, one of the last Spanish possessions in the Caribbean, was the subject of a brutal war between Spanish forces and Cubans who sought independence. After what became known as the Great War ended in 1878, Spain remained in control of Cuba, but again, the cost in financial terms and in respect of casualties was very high.

Thus, by the end of the nineteenth century, Spain retained only two significant overseas territories: Cuba and the Philippines. In both areas, Spain was facing opposition from the United States of America. Then, in 1898, the American cruiser USS *Maine* exploded and sank in harbor in Havana, Cuba. American newspapers claimed that this was sabotage deliberately carried out by the Spanish (though there is now doubt about whether this was true), and the phrase, "Remember the *Maine*! To hell with Spain!" became a rallying cry for Americans.

As a direct result, America declared war on Spain in April 1898 and began a blockade, cutting Cuba off from Spain. Meanwhile, in the Philippines, a naval battle in Manila Bay was decisively won by the U.S. Navy. This short war ended later in 1898 with the signature of the Treaty of Paris. This treaty forced Spain to give up sovereignty over Cuba and also ceded control over Puerto Rico, Guam, and the Philippines to the United States. The signing of this treaty effectively ended the Spanish Empire and established the United States for the first time as a significant international power.

The only overseas territory left to Spain after her war with America was in North Africa. In 1893, Spanish troops had occupied territory in this region, and in 1911, control of Morocco was formally divided between Spain and France. Spanish military forces in Morocco suffered a major military defeat in 1921 following the Rif Rebellion, but Morocco did not finally become independent until the 1950s. Now, Spain retains control over the cities of Ceuta and Melilla in North Africa and the Canary Islands off the west coast of Africa. These are the only lingering relics of the once mighty Spanish Empire.

Conclusion

Few empires in history were larger or left a longer-lasting cultural and linguistic legacy than the Spanish Empire. In the sixteenth and seventeenth centuries, this empire made Spain one of the richest and most powerful nations in the world, and it became the subject of envy amongst the other great powers. In 1738, English poet Samuel Johnson neatly summed up the wonder and jealousy that the Spanish provoked: "Has heaven reserved, in pity to the poor, No pathless waste or undiscovered shore, No secret island in the boundless main, No peaceful desert yet unclaimed by Spain?"

The Spanish Empire, and particularly the bullion that flowed from the Americas to Spain, brought massive change, but its very nature also brought hubris and the seeds of later problems. There was so much gold and silver flowing into Spain that there seemed no need to develop indigenous industries or improve agriculture. If anything was needed, it could simply be bought abroad and shipped to Spain. Even soldiers and military hardware could be purchased as required and used to protect the empire and extend it further.

Particularly under Habsburg rule, there seemed to be no consideration that this bullion was not inexhaustible. Massive debts were incurred on the assumption that they could be repaid using future imports of gold and silver. But armies of occupation and conquest are ruinously expensive to maintain, and when the supply of bullion from the Americas began to falter, the true state of the Spanish economy was starkly revealed. By the late 1700s, the Spanish Empire was still one of the largest in the world. Just one hundred years later, it had all but ceased to exist. Although the Napoleonic Wars, the Carlist Wars, and other internal revolts certainly contributed to this, Spain's empire succumbed mainly to a failure to reinvest any of the wealth flowing from the Americas into the development of the nation itself.

Nevertheless, the legacy left by the Spanish Empire can be seen around the world today. Spanish is the second most spoken native language in the world, used by almost 500 million people. Only Mandarin Chinese is used by more people. Catholicism is the largest religion in the world today, principally due to the spread of this religion by Spanish explorers in South and Central America and the Philippines. The impact of the Spanish Empire can also clearly be seen in the food, music, architecture, and legal and political systems used in those countries. In return, those same Spanish explorers brought back to Europe for the first time things that have become part of the fabric of life there, including potatoes, chili peppers, tomatoes, tobacco, beans, and even chocolate.

The Spanish Empire introduced the world for the first time to the concept of globalization. Spain (and Portugal) explored new lands and established maritime trade routes that spanned the world and saw the shipment of goods east and west. The Spanish peso became the first global currency, as Spanish and European goods found their way to the Americas and the Philippines, while goods from those areas became commonplace in Europe and Asia.

Few empires have had such a lasting impact on the modern world as that created and maintained by Spain in the sixteenth, seventeenth, and eighteenth centuries. Next time that you consume chocolate or avocado or peanuts or strawberries, or even chew gum, take a moment to consider that these things only became widely available due to the mighty Spanish Empire.

Bibliography

Elliott, J. H. (2006). *Empires of the Atlantic World: Britain and Spain in America 1492–1830.*

Elliott, J. H. (1960). *Imperial Spain: 1469-1716.*

Kamen, H. (2003). *Empire: How Spain Became a World Power, 1492-1763.*

Thomas, H. (2002). *Rivers of Gold: The Rise of the Spanish Empire from Columbus to Magellan.*